Fulfilled and Worthy!

Increase self-love, develop healthy personal relationships, and appreciate guilt free boundaries.

ANGEL TENNELLE

When you love yourself, it's easy to show others how to love you. -Angel

@2023 Angel Tennelle

ISBN : 979-8-9874010-0-2

ISBN ebook 979-8-9874010-1-9

All rights reserved

www.angeltennelle.com

Acknowledge: Photo by: Jodie Smith

Acknowledge: Editors: Deondra Pardue, Dr. Joel Boyce

For free resources, please visit www.fulfilledandworthy.com and join our email list.

I dedicate this book to my entire support group: My son, Traveontai, who is my biggest motivation in life and my bonus baby Destiny. My best friends who have been by my side through it all: Veleda, Deondra and Bridgett. My immediate family: my first best friend in life Jamie, my mom Peggy, who shows up everytime, my personal comedian and brother, Tory, and my daddy who is in heaven, James. My God daughters, who love me unconditionally: Kayden, MaKaylee, Sydney. My Godparents: Flora and Richard, and my church family for all the prayers Mt. Zion #228. Nothing in my life is possible without God.

Seeking assistance is not a sign of weakness, it's recognizing an area you're looking to improve in. -Angel

Drowning out the voices or ignoring the signs won't make the problem go away. It makes you deal with it longer.

-Angel

Contents

Foreword: vii
    By Deondra Pardue vii
Introduction: ix
Chapter: 1 1
    "No One Can Know" 1
Chapter 2 15
    "Okay, It Happened…Now what?" 15
Chapter 3 31
    "What They Gon' Do?" 31
Chapter 4 41
    "Pressure Release" 41
Chapter 5 49
    "Let's Heal" Forgiving it's healing 49
Chapter 6 59
    "Gotta Love Me" Self love journey 59

Chapter 7 75

"Happily Moving Forward" How to maintain in this space
....75

Closing/Epilogue: 85

Acknowledge, Activate, Attain & Align. Becoming
Fulfilled & Worthy! 89

*Live loud, live bold, live unapologetically. What they gon'
do? -Angel*

Foreword:

By Deondra Pardue

I am so relieved that this book is finally out! There are so many of you who will laugh, cry, and evoke much emotion because of the content in this book. When I first met Angel, I was a young tenderoni in college. I looked up to her in every aspect of life. I had no idea that we would become lifelong friends, and I also never thought that I could be so connected to another human being. She is the ying to my yang. I have witnessed so much growth in her mentally, financially, spiritually, and in her motherhood. As we age, we become closer. I admire Angel so much and now the world will be able to get a small glimpse of what I have witnessed for almost twenty years. I am also grateful for my best friend, and I am thankful to God that He uses her the way he does. If you are just now picking up this book…your life will not be the same. You're welcome in advance.

Patching things and emotions are temporary; healing things and emotions are permanent.

- Angel

Introduction:

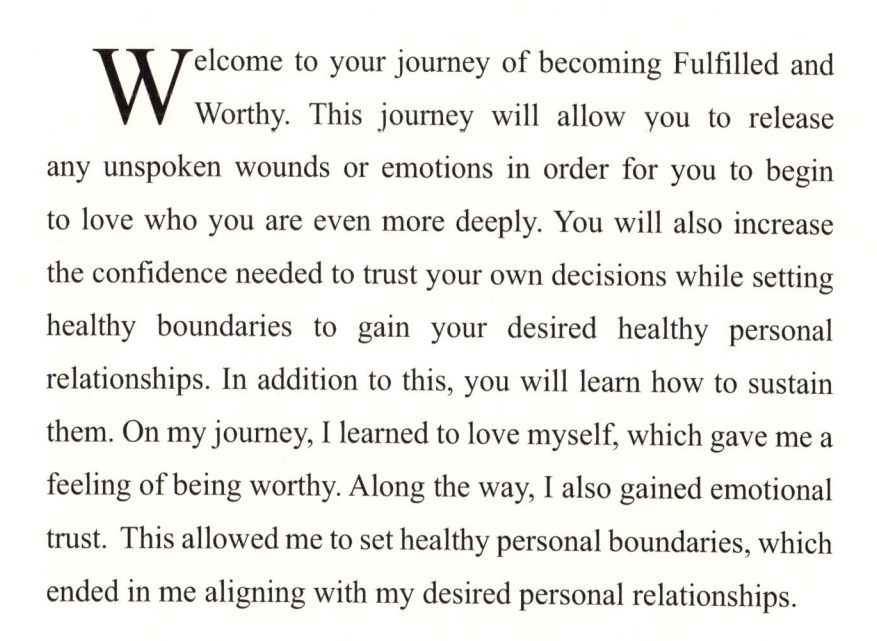

Welcome to your journey of becoming Fulfilled and Worthy. This journey will allow you to release any unspoken wounds or emotions in order for you to begin to love who you are even more deeply. You will also increase the confidence needed to trust your own decisions while setting healthy boundaries to gain your desired healthy personal relationships. In addition to this, you will learn how to sustain them. On my journey, I learned to love myself, which gave me a feeling of being worthy. Along the way, I also gained emotional trust. This allowed me to set healthy personal boundaries, which ended in me aligning with my desired personal relationships.

I am a person who has suffered from childhood trauma, experienced unhappiness, and loneliness. I was always considered a strong, dependable person for everyone else, but I only felt valued at work. If you can relate to any of these feelings, then I know that you, too, can come out of your journey Fulfilled and Worthy. Some challenges that I faced along the way included; but not limited to: not wanting to feel alone as well as investing more in the relationships that I desired. These actions resulted in me doing undesirable amounts of work, which led to me feeling less than. This emptiness caused me to attract more unfulfilling personal relationships. By following the steps listed in the chapters to follow, I was able to overcome finding my voice. I found my voice by overcoming abandonment issues and learning how to love myself, which gave me emotional trust to choose myself. I came to a place where I finally feel fulfilled and worthy, and you can accomplish this too.

By going through the 4 A's (Acknowledge, Activate, Attain and Align), I was more intentional about daily routines, mirror work, journaling, finding my voice and walking in my authenticity. Prior to my journey, I would sleep late and lay in the bed hitting the alarm five or six times. Whereas now, I get up throughout the week generally at the same time each day. Now I get started on my morning routine regularly. Prior to this journey, I constantly made many excuses, and I would frequently second guess things that I was thinking or wanted to say.

I truly own my voice now. I'm going to say what I need to say without being disrespectful or rude. I will use my voice to express how I feel, however prior to this mindset, I would think of others before I thought of myself. I would put my concerns last versus now I make myself and my feelings a priority. I ask myself, "How does this make me feel?" "Do I really want to do that?" "What do I need?"

I previously wanted to go with the flow, or do things that may not have been my favorite thing to do. Being unsure of who I was and being unsure if I was good enough created concerns about belonging and ultimately being alone. My journey started when my marriage failed, and I had to be completely honest about what I was truly dealing with or as I would call it, my personal lifetime movie. That situation was when the changes started. Ultimately, the point of where I had no other choice was when I was forced to make a decision between doing something that would benefit me or being put out of my place of residence. I chose myself for the first time in my life. In that very moment, all of the other feelings, emotions, and self doubt tried to resurface. However, that one choice allowed me to face my fears. I'm loving myself, feeling worthy, owning my voice and personality while setting boundaries, all while enjoying healthy personal relationships.

As I have started to walk in my own voice, I see life now through a different lens. I am now able to truly walk in alignment with my purpose of helping others gain these same results. This past year I have written a book, started speaking, and began coaching others on how to get the same results. I started investing in myself, gained better personal relationships with my family/friends, and found a new life that I have been waiting on.

At the end of "Fulfilled & Worthy" gaining self-love and attracting desired healthy personal relationships, you will look at your life from a different perspective and feel fulfilled and worthy. Don't put off on Monday what you can get started today! As you complete each chapter, you will gain a new feeling of self value, self trust, and find your voice to align with your desired personal relationships. With great expectation comes change. It took me over 40 years to get to this point, but it's never too late to get started. You can do it, and I will see you at the end Fulfilled and Worthy. It's your turn! What are you waiting on? Get started on Chapter One, already!

Lots of love,

Angel Tennelle

Elevation is growing, growing is changing, and we should all be continually evolving. -Angel

Chapter: 1

"No One Can Know"

Bring out the microphones, karaoke machines, camcorders and camera phones because babyyy I've been giving the people what they want! I could have been a musical genius, but no one paid enough attention to me. I've been making up songs since a very young age. I would create songs expressing how I felt.

You see, one thing I am is creative, and I wouldn't want the Lord to take anything away from me...especially my hearing! My granddaddy was deaf, and he is one person who I admired greatly. When I didn't want to hear what people had to say, like my mama, then I tried everything to make sure I couldn't hear her. "Did you hear me calling yo name?" My mama would yell from the kitchen. So Ms.Creative right here had the bright idea that I wanted to be deaf like my granddaddy. If I can't hear people, then what will they say? Nothing, right? Well, I had the bright idea to start putting small objects inside my ear as deep as they would go in order to block out all of the sound. I just didn't want to hear so maybe the negative would just go away. It's actually funny when I think about it now. I wanted to feel a sense of relief from hearing or experiencing anything bad and being deaf would solve all of my problems in my mind.

So honey, I would sit in front of the TV staring and trying to imagine what words they were saying while my mama was still calling my name from the kitchen. When I filled my ears with popcorn kernels that were too small, they would fall out. I needed something larger. So babyyy, I put a pinto bean in there and it was a perfect fit! I pushed it in as far as I could. Success! I was finally deaf like granddaddy. Sounds were barely muffled, but I couldn't hear much overall.

So my mom finally came into the living room and said something like, "Girl you hear me calling ya name? I've been calling you. I know you ain't ignorin' me! What's wrong witchu, Angel? Angel? What's wrong and why can't you hear me?" After my deep silence, she finally realized that I actually couldn't hear her, and so off to the emergency room we went.

My nickname should have "ER" because I stayed in the ER from doing something crazy.

The doctor said, "Let's just clean her ears out. Let's flush out everything." When I tell you my mama was five shades of angry and she's a fairly light complected lady, so you could literally see her turning bright red like a tomato as they pulled out that pinto bean, along with a couple of popcorn kernels. My mom burst out in anger, "Why do you want to be deaf?" I don't know what my response was, but I'm pretty sure it wouldn't be the truth of me saying I didn't want to hear you. But that's just one of the little situations where I was really trying to let people know that I needed attention and they were attempting to fix the surface of what they saw, but never the root cause. The root cause was too much and none of us were adequately equipped for what life was going to bring us. And before you say something, I know I am not the only one who did stupid things for attention. What types of things did you do for attention?

Ain't life crazy? Well, allow me to let you in on my 'aha moments' while reflecting on my life, growth and other situations. I was thinking of other experiences that happened to me since a young age and how I got to the point where I am currently. I now realize that I was unintentionally asking, practically begging for help through my actions and more deliberately through my words. I chuckle now when I think about my experiences from the past. But thank God that I'm stronger now, and the memories don't send me back down a dark rabbit hole.

As a musical genius at the tender age of 6 or 7, I created a song to express how I felt because apparently no one was listening to much of anything I was saying, or maybe I didn't know the words to have the conversation. But I made a song about everything. One song that everyone remembers to this day was a short song that was sweet and to the point saying exactly what I was feeling. The song was called "No, nobody loves me."

The song goes like this: Nobody loves me. Nobody cares. Nobody loves me. So why am I even here?

I'm gonna say it again just so I can make sure that you understand that you read it right the first time:

Nobody loves me. Nobody cares. Nobody loves me. So why am I even here?

I sang that song so much that my immediate family knows every lyric to the song. When I do certain things, sometimes they'll sing it and say, "here she goes, again". They would sing, "Nobody loves me, nobody cares…". I do believe the song would fit the situation.

For example, on Christmas one year when I was in grade school, everybody else got what they wanted and asked for on their Christmas wish list. Everyone except for me. When I opened my gift, it was so obvious that the efforts were not there at all. The effort was put into my two siblings or my cousins. Me on the other hand, I would immediately feel like an outcast, isolated and different. The black sheep is what people say. After looking up at the joy in everyone else's eyes, I look down at my effortless gifts such as socks, oranges, nuts with a small toy; things that I really didn't want on Christmas. I would sit there and take a deep breath. I started singing my song "nobody loves me", and that was my way of saying that I recognize that I'm being treated differently without stating it directly. Can you imagine that? I was so young, but treated so differently. There's a saying that if you listen to people, they'll tell you how they feel. Either through words or actions, in my case it was a song. As an adult and processing what I was doing at such a young age, I realized that I knew that I was being treated unfairly. The emptiness led to me feeling an even deeper emotion; I felt abandoned.

Back in the day, family operated differently than it does now. People truly believe that it took a village to raise a child and I still believe that. During those times, if a girl birthed a child outside of wedlock and they were very young, then an older sister would typically take the child and raise him as if it was hers. At times she would completely claim the child as being hers. If the parents were not fit to raise a child for whatever reason, then the grandparents would take the kids and raise them. This is because the bigger picture was the well-being of the actual child or children. Some of the reason was also to keep people from feeling ashamed, as well as kids getting taken through the child custody system. No family wanted to experience the embarrassment of going through that process. Well, my siblings and I were in that predicament. Our parents couldn't raise us together, and it wasn't just because me and my siblings witnessed their divorce. My parents were not in a position to safely raise us or house us in an environment that would've been beneficial for us. So a village raised me and my siblings. The village would entail my grandparents, along with a host of cousins, aunts, uncles, and other relatives.

My grandparents were older than my classmates' grandparents. Granddaddy was still working at the time. Grandma was still keeping everybody else's kids because that was her passion. Grandma was an excellent cook and everyone knew it. Outside of raising other people's kids, she worked part time at the local school cafeteria cooking. I remember she would bring us snacks, such as soup, peanut butter cookies, and candy from school; she truly tried to help raise us as much as she could.

It was impossible for my grandparents to keep an eye on everything; we got away with quite a bit. At times, we would go back and forth with my mama when she could get us, but ultimately we always ended back in the residence of our grandparents or other relatives. Mama consistently tried to get us when she could, but my dad created a whole new family after divorcing my mom. His new wife had kids of her own; one boy and one girl around the same age as us. I referred to my step siblings as 'sister and brother' when we did see them. They seemed so happy. So ideal. So normal. So complete.

Can you imagine watching one parent mentally and financially struggling in every aspect of life while still doing all she can to help, while the other parent was completely capable? My mother never stopped loving my father and kept trying to make him happy from afar. Meanwhile, my father created a great environment with his new wife; they had a home, great jobs, and a seemingly perfect life.

All I felt was abandonment.

There were three of us, and no one seemed to want us. In my young mind if your parents, the ones that created you and birthed you, didn't want you, then who else would? If my parents don't love me, then who will? Were we as kids to blame for my parent's divorce? Why didn't they want us? Why couldn't they just get back together and make us a happy family again?

Now I understand that they loved us the best way they knew how, but at the time that's all I felt. These are some of the questions that were going through my mind. I felt the abandonment, then later came the abuse.

I was being taken advantage of sexually by male cousins and uncles. My parents didn't realize that they left us in the hands of several abusers. My grandparents were doing the best that they could to provide love and support in a limited capacity. However, they were busy. As a child, I couldn't process right from wrong, good from bad, nor my 'yes's from my 'no's when the abuse took place. I knew it didn't feel right, and I felt dirty. Why did this happen to me? Am I the only one experiencing this? Should I tell someone? Will anyone believe me? Could I have prevented this from happening to me? Will I get kicked out of the family? I remember these experiences from childhood that led me to feel abused, abandoned, and isolated. I became angry and this anger carried over into my adulthood.

Since I experienced the feeling of abandonment, abuse, and isolation, I tried to prevent these things from happening to innocent people the best way I knew how. I assumed the role of protector of all things that I loved. There were several instances where I would get into a fist fight with boys who said anything about my siblings. I had something to prove. I was always afraid to fight girls because of the damage that I felt that I would do to them. I couldn't control my anger back then. As I have gotten older, I've realized the impact that words and actions can have. Words matter. Actions that we take matter. I would sing songs and try to spend the night at my cousins or friend's house to try to bury the pain as well as the reality that my life was not ideal as an adolescent. I had no security.

The things that are instilled in you as a child, whether right or wrong, good, bad, or indifferent tend to stick with most. Some refer to them as family traits or curses. Think about that for a minute. What family curses are you trying to break? What are some practices that you do that were learned from your childhood and never went away?

When my parents got a divorce my baby sister took it extremely hard. I was told that it was my sole responsibility to take care of my baby sister as well as my older brother. At the time, I didn't really think about it. All they got was a yes ma'am or yes sir. I'm pretty sure it was a yes ma'am in this case.

"Ya'll don't separate, you understan' me? Now take care of you, take care of them, and do not separate. You take good care of 'em." These are the words that were shared with me as a child growing up after my parents got a divorce. So no matter what happens, it's my responsibility to make sure my siblings are good and that we are close knit, we stick together, we don't separate, and that's exactly what I did. As the middle child, this made me feel a sense of purpose. I felt my older brother was the boy who had a special place in my parent's heart. My baby sister was the baby girl who could get anything she wanted. I was in the middle. As I've gotten older and reflected, I come to realize that perhaps my parents knew that I could handle situations and they considered me to be the backbone of the group. Both my siblings are amazing humans, and I am so grateful for our connection to this day.

Particularly with my sister, there was a time we were briefly living with my dad and his wife and children. I was maybe a freshman in high school at this time. I recall a box fan of some sort being broken. Okay, it was only a box fan; the kind that many people back then put in windows. My sister was instantly blamed for breaking the box fan.

I instantly went into protection mode and she was seconds away from getting a whoopin' from my daddy. The fact was that the box fan was indeed broken, but no one actually saw her break it. I saw my sister beginning to tear up and that was not permitted in my eyes. I remember being told that crying is a sign of weakness as a young adolescent. We were specifically taught to never allow someone to see you cry. This is not to say that you are not allowed to curry overall; however, no one is allowed to see you. Thankfully I know now that crying is healthy and gives you a release. But it was instilled to me that you don't let anybody see you cry because you are strong. Just suck it up. My daddy was so upset about this fan being broken, and he approached my sister. I bucked up to him before he could yell and whoop at my sister, and I said, "My sister is not getting a whoopin' today for the fan being broken because no one saw her break it." I puffed my chest up even more and told her to get behind me. As you can tell, I have a mouth on me. I've always had a loud and smart, bold mouth. My smart mouth is better maintained now than what it used to be, but at that age, I didn't care what would come next from my daddy. My daddy was so pissed off that he could spit fire; enough to burn the entire house down! But I stood my ground. I remember him yelling at me, "You act just like your damn mama!". To me, that was a huge compliment. I still will take it as a compliment to this day because my mama is amazing.

My daddy then grabs the belt even tighter and begins to give me a whoopin'. I am sure he was raging more from the fact that his small teenage daughter was ready to face him like a grown man. He thought he had a point to prove, well, so did I.

When I tell you that I was standing there taking each and every strike of the belt without making a sound while staring at my daddy directly and fiercely in his eyes, as if I was communicating to him that his hits do not even phase me. I absolutely refused to cry. I stared and stared at him. Talk about stubborn, chile! I knew I had to stand up to him or he would win the battle. I needed to protect my sister to the point that I would take the punishments on her behalf. After the sixth or seventh strike from my daddy, all of a sudden the belt buckle of the belt ended up hitting me in my face. I believe we both were in shock at that point. My sister began screaming in fear and crying profusely. He paused for what seemed like ten minutes, but more like ten seconds. He then slowly lowered the belt, let out a big sigh, and he slowly walked away. He gave up. I won. I defeated him. That was the last time he ever struck me.

When I think about these situations that happened, I reflect on how insubordinate and at times terrible I was as a child. But I also knew what made me terrible, right? I was a product of my environment. I remember when my daddy walked away and my sister was so scared, bless her heart. I did not cry, y'all… like hardly ever. I'm telling you that not crying was instilled in me so much that I don't think that I allowed my son to see me cry for the first time until I lost my grandparents as a grown woman. I wouldn't even allow my sister to cry if she was getting a whoopin', and for the most part-she didn't cry much either aloud. She would bury her face in a pillow after getting a whoopin'. "They don't get the privilege of seeing you cry. You stay strong."

Times when I had every right to cry, I didn't cry. I remember staring at myself in the mirror wishing a tear would fall, but it just wouldn't happen. I think back to several instances in my marriage where I probably should;ve cried profusely. I went through a lot when I was married. Even with all the craziness that I went through within my marriage, I didn't want anyone to see me cry because of the old thought that I was told that I shouldn't.

This belief was instilled in me by my grandparents, likely from their ancestors from slavery days (I think). I taught my son the same thing until I learned that was terrible advice. Let's just be real. What you know is what you produce and how you handle things. These old beliefs put so much weight on me for so many years and I owned it. I walked in. I lived it. I didn't complain about it. I did it. I didn't realize that my thought process was jeopardizing me.

I remained a protector. My siblings depended on me for many things. They knew that if they needed something, then it was done in my eyes. If I got paid, I always threw them some change. If I had it, then they did too. I was the backbone because that is what I was taught to do, and it made me who I am today. I don't want to say 'strong' because I don't think that it made me strong per se, however it equipped me to handle situations differently than most. My experiences made me hurt more overall because I was hurting alone. I felt empty. Thank God for growth.

To my sister, I didn't know any better when I was younger. I'm sorry, sweetheart.

To my son. My apologies. I was broken. I felt unworthy. I was not fulfilled.

Due to not feeling fulfilled and suffering in silence, I made some unwise decisions in my life. However, I learned to grow from them. I needed to internally acknowledge what was happening. During the silent painful times throughout my life when I needed a release, acknowledgement is the foundation that would've helped me greatly. I learned to outwardly express that I felt unwanted and unloved, as well as the desire to be accepted. I wanted to assist everyone, however, withholding information led to unhealthy relationships, instead of good relationships, with my family. Now that I have fully internally acknowledged the issues that I had in the past, I focus on prayer and meditation to assist me.

Who I was, what I am: Self Awareness

- I assumed that I was alone because I could not SEE anyone that I could relate to
- Growing up feeling abandoned, made me not trust or allow anyone to be more than transnational in my life
- At the age of 46, I am in a space of owning my voice and walking in who I am. I wanted to be confident in feeling appreciated and enough by walking in my truth

FREE resource: go to www.fulfilledandworthy.com select the free resource, tab click Chapter 1.

Chapter 2

"Okay, It Happened...Now What?"

Acknowledge it happened. Denial is real.

Many times we want to block things out and push them to the back of our mind as if it never happened. We ask ourselves, "How could this happen to me?" Or we say, "This wasn't supposed to happen!" Or maybe even, "I must have been dreaming."

I came to realize that it was only hurting me trying to deny, hide or ignore the truth; it doesn't make it go away. Denial or simply refusing to admit your truth or accepting the reality of something that you feel or see as unpleasant is a very bad place to be. When I started to see that bad things didn't appear to be bothering anyone else, I knew that something had to change.

The first time I felt comfortable enough to talk to someone about my experiences was when I was in middle school, and I had a boyfriend that I felt comfortable enough to talk to. It wasn't the most pleasant state in our lives. We both had some situations that we were dealing with regarding our unstable and unsafe living environments, feelings of abandonment, and that we both felt we had to carry the burdens of our immediate family members. We had each other. This made me feel as if he could relate to situations that I had been through even though I am a female and he is a male. I trusted him. I can remember telling him stories of things that happened to me not too detailed or explicit, but enough for him to get the picture. I remember him sharing some of his feelings, and things that he was dealing with as well. Some nights we would just cry together. It was okay to cry with him because no one would know. I know he wouldn't tell anyone that I could cry. We had a very strong bond and this made us grow closer and it was a safe space. After being able to have those conversations with him and tell my truth with me not feel judged, or looked down upon was a very healthy practice for me at the moment. I thought I was going to marry this boy; I was so in love.

I remember thinking I wanted to talk to other people about my abuse, but questions would come up. Like, is it safe to share this? How do I really feel about this? Can I put this into words? Do I even want to share this? Will they even listen? Are they going to tell somebody else? What does this say about me? Where do I go from there? Is this affecting my actions?

These were just some of the questions that came to me when I was thinking about talking to other people. Here it is 20 plus years later that a friend reached out to me via social media and it was really good to catch up. It was like we never missed a beat. The trust was still there. The friendship was still there. That was a very, very good feeling to have. I brought many childhood practices into my adulthood.

Being a prideful person can make you block your own blessings. At times I wish I could go back and smack myself in the head; however, I live with no regrets and I like to say that I have learned from the past. There are situations that I should have let go a long time ago, but pride kicked in. Y'all, I was in a whole marriage that was failing miserably in almost every aspect. Aside from the many factors of why it was failing miserably, I specifically remember one distinct day when I had no choice but to swallow my pride because I was literally losing my mind. I couldn't hold up the pride any longer.

At the time, my then husband and I were together for approximately eleven or twelve years, but married the last four years out of this span. I was internalizing all of the gut feelings of mistold truths, blatant lies, and deceitfulness that I had become accustomed to. I was to blame for everything from his perspective and was being mentally controlled. He didn't win all the battles, but he wanted to control how I dressed, how I wore my hair, the jewelry I put on, the friends I could have, and anything else that dealt with image. I was staying in the marriage depressed and lifeless on the inside. I stayed because that is what I was taught to do from my grandma, and I didn't want to divorce like my parents did. My son had a father figure in the house even though he was not a person that I should have stayed with for such a long time. He was good to my son, and that overpowered my desire to consider walking away from the relationship. At the time, I felt as if there were only two things that I knew how to do well, and that was being a mother and excelling in my career. Being a perfect wife was nowhere in my deck of cards. Have you ever stayed in a relationship for the wrong reasons? Were you ever viewed at work as having the 'perfect life' at home, but it was actually miserable? Well, that was me.

This one particular day, I was laying on my bed in the house that consisted of my one and only blood son and my husband. He had other children who would come stay with us from time to time. My son and step daughter were graduating from high school, and I wanted to create a slideshow of pictures for a picnic we planned on having the next day. He would always demand that I not touch his items, and I wouldn't. However, this one particular day, I was on a time constraint and I needed to quickly grab pictures to complete the task at hand. Therefore, I grabbed my husband's hard drive with the goal of finding older pictures of our two graduating children, and I was in no way prepared to see what my eyes witnessed.

They were everywhere. I was in a literal state of shock. I saw pictures and videos from my house, my bedroom, my couch, her house, hotels, vacations, etc. from years back from that point. At four years into our marriage, the cheating had to have started at least two years prior to saying I do. My husband was living a double life with another woman for about 6 years; someone who I never thought he would even consider sexually.

I instantly saw red. I was numb.

The feeling that I felt is a feeling that too many spouses feel who don't deserve that feeling. I hated it. I couldn't remember the last time I felt so much hurt at that point in my life. I gave him everything and more. He didn't deserve to be treated so well with how he treated me as a spouse.

Without fully processing what was going on, I instantly called my husband while he was at work. He answered innocently as he had no idea of what had just transpired. After he heard my rage he quickly hung up the phone. So I drove to his job. I needed answers right then. This couldn't wait until he got home from work. He was a very prideful person who didn't want the public to know anything negative could ever occur in his life or our lives as a married couple. From the outside looking in, our lives looked perfect.

I grabbed my keys, hopped in my car, drove to his job and walked right in. I demanded to speak to him while literally shaking. I informed them that it was an emergency and I needed him right at that moment. I saw him cut the corner and we locked eyes. He knew that I was hot. He instantly tried to calm me down, but all I could do was lash out and scream, "What the hell is going on? After I paid for everything and did everything for you. Years and years of you fucking another bitch! You're fucking that white bitch you worked with? You are so fucking low down! You fucking other bitches at this job too?" I was literally screaming. As I said earlier, I had a mouth on me.

He kept trying to calm me down by offering to escort me to my vehicle and away from his job. As we were walking out, I knew he was scrambling trying to come up with the best excuse he could. He tried to convince me that it wasn't what it looked like, and he gave many excuses and that infuriated me even more. Eventually I calmed down enough to leave and go back home, but on that long ride home I just kept thinking about how life was going to be when he got off work and back to the house.

He was a smooth talker, the kind of person who could manipulate anyone to do anything for him. He could sell water to the ocean. I wasn't going to let him sweet talk himself out of this one. While riding back home, it all hit me like a ton of bricks as I reflected on this woman and their infidelity. This woman was a "family friend" who would come to our family barbecues sometimes. She eventually stopped and I didn't think anything of it. I also remembered the night that I married this man, she called him repeatedly that evening non-stop. Mr. 'Good with words' somehow convinced me that she was fine and the phone calls were random back on our wedding night. Have you ever known that someone was lying to you and you just allowed the lie to move forward? That's what I did. I ignored all the signs.

When I pulled up at home, I thought about how I couldn't let the world know what happened and be exposed to such embarrassment. I allowed my pride to take over. The kids were at the house by the time he got back from work. "Suck it up buttercup" is what I told myself repeatedly. We have an event tomorrow and we need to pretend that everything is just fine for the sake of our kids. This is how I handled most of our stressful situations. I concluded that this situation was just another messed up part of how my life was supposed to be. I didn't feel worthy enough to be in a happy marriage at the time. I chose to marry him, so I thought I had to deal with what marriage came with. Boy, was I wrong.

I wasn't a push over by any means. I demanded to see the mistress face to face the next day after the event concluded. I demanded that he drive me to her house so I could confront her. I had no intention of getting into a physical altercation, I simply wanted her to face me directly. On the drive there he kept coming up with excuses of why we shouldn't go and we were arguing. We were in his pick up truck, he had pride in that truck. We were on the interstate driving at least 70 miles per hour. I told him to take me to this woman's house and he said a smart comment back to me. Before he could finish the smart comment, I threw the gear from drive to park causing the truck to swerve.

"Are you trying to kill us both?" He yelled. I yelled louder, "I don't care about that right now, take me to that bitch's house and I don't want to hear anything else about it!" He dreadfully drove me there.

When we pulled up, she instantly started screaming that she was going to call the police. I was confused because I didn't threaten her nor raise my voice. She likely projected her guilt out and tried to deal with the situation as best as she could. She then started screaming at him, "I can't believe you put me in this shit you asshole! I hate you!"

We left. That was the longest drive back to my house as we were in complete silence the entire way there. I was trying to process everything that I could as quickly as I could. So many mixed emotions were going through my mind. I imagined what life would be like without him. I knew I couldn't murder him and get away with it, I didn't want to go to hell. If I knew I wouldn't go to hell, then I am not sure what I would've done. Thank God for deliverance.

It was the day of the event and everyone showed up, even his ex-wife. The event took place at our house. As if I needed any more women that my ex-husband previously slept with to tamper with my emotions, his ex wife also seemed to want to pick with me on this particular day. She would go around the house and make humming noises as she looked at our family pictures and refrigerator magnets with chore lists on them. "That little thing is cute. This little photo is cute. Hmmmmm, I guess that's cute too." She mustered. Little did she know, I was doing everything I could to make it through the day. I prayed that I could contain my actions throughout this event. I didn't know how to feel, I didn't feel at all. Thankfully my sister made this situation comical with small inside jokes. Eventually I shared concerns with my husband and he handled the situation. She was cordial the rest of the event, thankfully. We made it through the event. My husband and I went through many obstacles after that; there's not enough pages in this book to go through them all.

I blamed myself for how I ended up where I was for a while. There was so much pressure on being perfect and living this pretend life. When I went back to work to face reality the next day after visiting the mistress, I remember sitting there and reflecting on everything that happened. The load was so much, and then I knew that I had to try my best to be 'normal' at work. I worked at a financial institution where my job was to call people and ask them to catch up on their payments. The job was mentally exhausting at times due to the nature and responsibilities of the job itself.

As I stated, this particular day was my first day back to work after finding out about the infidelity. Having all of this inside of me, I didn't feel like actually working. I remember my boss at the time was a younger lady who was just trying to do her job. She requested that I call someone, and I straight up told her, "No, I'm not doing it!" I walked out. Bless her heart, I was taking out my frustration on her. She didn't deserve that, but all the pressure and frustration that I was holding in at the time was unbearable. I was prideful and needed a release.

After I stormed out of my job, I started taking a walk. Tears were flowing from my face uncontrollably. I wasn't accustomed to crying, therefore I knew that this was a serious bodily uncontrollable function. I couldn't let anyone see me! I was on a major local road and I felt that the chances of someone seeing me were great. I refused to let anyone see me walking down the street, so I went to a nearby neighborhood and began hiding behind bushes when cars drove by. I couldn't let anyone see me. If I thought the homeowner could see me, then I even ducked and dodged them from bush to bush. I realized that I couldn't keep doing this. What if these people had a dog or spiders? I am upset, but I am not trying to get bitten.

"This is crazy!" I thought to myself. I didn't have transportation for whatever reason this particular day; I'm not sure if my car was in the shop or what. I couldn't compose myself any longer. I had a full meltdown. I hit rock bottom. I knew I needed to contact those who are closest to me.

I called my childhood best friend who has been by my side my entire life. I could barely get any words out. I was crying profusely. She immediately knew something was terribly wrong because of the tears and my voice. I've been a shower and closet crier my whole life because no one could see me cry there. She was alarmed and immediately called her husband. I didn't know it at the time, but she was making arrangements to come to me. She and her husband lived about 3 hours away. I then wanted to call my local best friend, but I am nine years older than her and I knew she looked up to me. I didn't want her to see me in this state. I was too prideful to call her.

I then called my sister and begged her to come pick me up. I stressed to her to come alone without her husband or kids. I needed her more than she realized at this point. She came, but when I opened the car door, I saw her children in the back. I was so upset. I knew she tried to not bring them, but she was just trying to physically get to me.

Time flew by because when I got home, my childhood best friend showed up for me. I needed them and they were there for me. When I saw my childhood best friend, I was overwhelmed with even more emotions because she literally showed up for me. That caring gesture was one of the most meaningful things that I have witnessed in my entire life. I mattered to her. She was ready; gun loaded and everything. Good thing she didn't have to use it. If you don't have a friend like that or build the relational capacity with friends you have now because everyone needs someone like that in their lives. We talked, laughed and even cried. She called my local best friend and she showed up for me as well. I didn't know what it would look like, but I knew that I couldn't continue to be with my husband in the long run. I tried the best way I could to say as long as I could. However, eventually a couple years later my husband and I finally divorced.

Some of my takeaways that I learned: I am not responsible for what happened to me. I can let go of it. Let go of the self blame. Often I would think of the saying "People can only do what you allow them to," and I can remember thinking, but I didn't allow it. I couldn't or didn't know how to stop it. It happened anyway and this is not fair. I wasn't strong enough in my mind. I felt ashamed that I allowed these horrific things to happen to me. I am so glad that I know better. None of it was my fault. Not one situation was my fault.

Have you ever been in a room by yourself that felt like you've had a million eyes watching you? That's how I used to feel when I was holding on to all of the things afraid of judgment, even though I knew I couldn't change what happened to me. It didn't matter if I was a nicer person, it didn't matter if I was a good kid or a bad kid. It did not matter. I even tried to think about different scenarios or play them out in my head. Well, maybe if I was happier, or maybe if I was lighter skinned, or if my hair was curly. Maybe if I made more money or maybe if I didn't have as strong of a personality then I would be loved more. But what I realized shortly after those thoughts is that none of those things truly mattered. It didn't matter what I looked like. It didn't matter what kind of attitude I had. I tried controlling all of these things that just did not matter. I came to the conclusion that there was nothing that I could have done that would have changed the outcome. If anything that happened to me, I know I can't say speaking up could have prevented it from going on so long either. But that's not what happened. I was afraid of being blamed. I would think that it would be my fault for things that came afterwards, such as breaking up the family. I thought it was my responsibility to keep the family together as a child, as well as in my blended family.

The reality of it is that I just had to realize that nobody deserved to judge me, but me and the Lord. It was all self blaming. It was me trying to hold myself accountable for other people's actions as time would have it. I learned through living life that self blame only makes it worse. Trying to figure out why someone did something or hold myself accountable for what someone did to me was not my responsibility. My blaming myself only kept me in a bad space.

Some of the healing practices that I did to help get to a point where I could share what was happening to me with others was rehearsing the conversations in the mirror, writing down what I was holding in, writing down how it made me feel, or writing why I felt weak because of what happened to me. After I wrote all that down, I would turn around and I would write down things that made me feel good about myself. I had to allow myself to feel what I felt. I would create good songs about myself instead of the ones about being mistreated and lonely. I accepted who I was. I realized that I had the power to rewrite my story. I have a blank sheet of paper to start creating a new story. I can make my story be whatever I wanted it to be because I have control of my actions.

I had to openly and externally acknowledge that it was okay. Even at a young age, my boyfriend was able to be there for me by simply listening and connecting to me. My best friends and my sister allowed me to externally acknowledge what was going on by taking the time to listen to me and then show up for me. Nowadays, I have professional counselors who allow me to externally acknowledge what has transpired in my life through talking to them. I had to externally acknowledge that unfortunate situations happened to me, and I had to talk about it. When I openly share these unfortunate occurrences, it helps me pull myself out of the self sabotage mindset that I had unintentionally. We all are the authors of our own books; we can't change the past, but we actually have a big voice in how our future will be. We know how to externally acknowledge what has transpired to us; we have to be bold enough to speak outwardly about it. You, too, can externally acknowledge the past with plans to move forward.

What happened to me IS NOT me: Self Love

- I was ashamed of what I was going through which I became too prideful. Now I am translucent and resilient.

- I used to think what happened to me DEFINED me, but it does not.

- To deny, hide, or ignore what has happened does not make it false.

FREE resource: go to www.fulfilledandworthy.com select the free resource tab, click Chapter 2.

Chapter 3

"What They Gon' Do?"

ACTIVATE

Accepting your truth when your heart needs a little more time is challenging. I believe that our hearts activate our minds, and our hearts heal faster than our minds as well. We have to get to the point where we are willing to face reality and be okay with knowing that things happened in the past, then will see things in a different perspective. I have never known how to accurately express myself without being angry; therefore, I had so much frustration, disappointment, and confusion bottled up inside of me. I held my truth in for so long feeling unworthy and unlovable, and I didn't want to let anyone see that I felt that way. I felt that I had to hide it. So I pushed everything else to the side and decided to excel where I could, which was in my work life.

My family was all that I knew. I was so afraid of how they would react, and I can recall being told by one of my beloved ones that, "what goes on in this house, stays in his house." That mindset made me afraid to tell anybody. I am a very literal person, and my understanding of that saying was that I better not tell a soul what is going on inside of this house. Period. I can remember, well, "What they gon' do?" My boogie man. I thought about if I told anything, then will my family blame me? Will my family disown me? How will this affect my quality of life? Will my child get made fun of? Then, it hit me. Not everyone is going to believe me. Even if they didn't believe me, my mindset and motto was-and still is- "what they gon' do?" This is a staple phrase of mine because no one can take your voice unless you give it to them. I made my own choice not to speak up and being silent was still the action. Right? I mean, it may not be the right action, but it was still action.

That was when I truly started to learn that I was my own worst enemy. I was so worried about everybody else and their opinions. What they gon' say? What they gon' do? How are they gon' move? What are they gon' say behind my back? What they want? Just what, what, what, what, what? All of these 'whats' were causing me to be so miserable. I was so ashamed of being miserable that no one knew that I actually was miserable.

I think my hesitation to own my voice in the space was just as detrimental to me as the things that actually happened to me. The things that happened to me only happened for a moment. What I was doing to myself, was happening for as long as it was, in my mind, half of a lifetime, or shall I say half of my lifetime. By me not accepting my truth sooner, caused me so many silent issues in my adulthood. I was in mistreated relationships and looking for love in all the wrong places.

A chain reaction of what was actually happening to me was hidden because of the feeling that no one cared about me. The feeling of feeling abandoned. When you walk into this space of, "I don't care" or when you hit rock bottom, then you question what matters. Not much seems to matter anymore. That is when I owned the, "what they gon' do" attitude. My perspective changed.

I came to realize that I'm just as valid as the next person. I decided to walk in my truth. I decided that I was going to start to have a life of no regrets. I was no longer going to suffer in silence. I will journal and find out what my truth is while allowing it to come from a good place. The more I was able to say, "what they gon' do?" and walk in whatever action that I needed to in that moment were the moments that I really started to break the on-going self blame cycle.

When I think about different aspects of my life , what mattered most was how much I believed in myself and in my abilities. Now, I have a God baby and I call her Syd Syd and her name is Sydney Howard. Syd has a Tic Tok account. When I open up my Tik Tok app, she's always at the top and typically one of the first people to pop up. When I tell y'all, my baby is there living her best life. She's got the confidence to do anything. She doesn't care how it looks. She doesn't care about who has to say what. She doesn't care, and I used to have that same mindset as a child.

Somewhere along my way, I started caring too much about other people's opinions. Somebody said something to me that made me care about how things looked and how things were presented so much that I would alter my initial desires. I started second guessing everything. I'm still very much myself because I can't hide my personality. However, somewhere along the way, I started caring about the stuff that makes me pause. I've been pausing on so much stuff it is unreal. Now the other part is that I believe that it's the devil trying hard to keep me from my blessings.

Here's the thing, my best friend, Deondra Pardue, is part of my best friend trio. She tells me all the time to "do it afraid", which is a book and phrase she's heard from Joyce Meyers, as well as a prior coworker. Deondra encourages me to attack everything that gives me fear with that "do it afraid" mindset. But what I kept thinking and reflecting on is that I'm not afraid to actually do things, but my fear comes from what people are going to say. When I realized that, then the phrase hit me differently. I'm not afraid to do a lot. I don't fear the action of completing things. I've never been afraid. If you know me, you know I walk in it. I'm gon' say what I need to say as respectfully as I can and as professionally as I can when I'm in those environments. I'm gon' do what I need to do, and everything comes from a place of good intentions.

However, the more I started to reflect on it, I didn't want to admit to it! I was truly afraid of what people were going to say. I didn't want them to judge me. Shut up, y'all! That's a whole new mindset, right? I have all of these catchphrases, you know, I love to say that catchphrases are my thing. Well, one of my favorite sayings is, "What they gon' do"? Here's the thing, while I was saying it, I wasn't realizing that was the one thing that I truly needed to tell myself. I needed to digest this.

I came to the realization that at times when people are talking to you, they're really talking themselves through that same situation or they're telling you how they wished they handled the situation. We have power and should use it! It's okay with what they say because guess what? "What they gon' do?" Huh? "What they gon' do?"

I had to internalize that to, "What am I gon' do?" Oh, "That'll talk!" (This is another one of my catch phrases y'all can use if you want to). But what they gon' do sometimes determines what you gon' do. You ain't in control of anybody else in this lifetime, but yourself, not your parents, not your kids (as much as we like to control them and tell them what to do.) Now we can guide them and teach them, but that's another story for another book on another day. Don't worry about it. I'm gonna let y'all know. But right now, it's, "what you gon' do?" Where are you at right now? Where you want to be and what you gon' do? And what you gon' do may not look like what somebody else does.

That's when you have to start reflecting. You have to start asking yourself those uncomfortable questions. I mean, going through it. I can't tell y'all how I will man, I will shut down. Do you understand me? I like to get in my quiet place. I hear God better when I'm in my quiet place. I don't have any distractions. You will frequently hear me say that when God created me he gave me two scoops of joy. Alright? Most people don't know how to handle one scoop. What they gon' do with two? It doesn't matter what they gon' do. What matters more is what am I gon' do with these two scoops of joy? Guess what? I'm gonna sprinkle a little here, and I'll sprinkle a little there. I'm gon' to sprinkle it everywhere because that's why He gave it to me.

I allowed what I thought other people were thinking to tone me down. "Angel, you doin' way too much. You too extra. Here she go wit that. Oh my goodness, Ms. Extra!" My response? You are right! I am extra and if you don't like it, then keep scooting, boo! I didn't want to be alone because I was alone. What I should have recognized is that being alone was where I could find my healing. Being alone was where I would find my purpose. Being alone was where I could grow. I didn't know that! All I knew was, "Lord I don't want to be alone, don't nobody love me. Don't nobody care, Lord where is my Boaz, can I just get a "Bo"? We can make him the "az" together, right? I didn't curse y'all, I promise! But, this is what I wanted. I desired companionship so bad y'all I settled for oooo weee, I don't even want to talk about how badly I settled. But if y'all ask me I will...maybe. I hope you're taking notes because I'm giving y'all some real tips out here. Y'all heard me? I'm sprinkling real 'Angel drops' on y'all. Or better yet, let me say I'm dropping some feathers. Okay? It's okay. I know to share, I know to share. I want y'all to realize that at the end of it nothing else in life matters, but what y'all gon' do.

When it comes to dating, sadly... I was molested, I was raped as a child. This negatively impacted my dating life. "What they gon' do?" Either they like me or they don't. If they don't, it's their loss because I am amazing. But I didn't feel that way until I got the "what they gon' do?" kind of attitude.

So what if your cousin doesn't talk to you? I mean, is your life gonna end? Do you live with them? Is it somebody you got to see every single day? If you don't talk to them at the family reunion, then you will lose no sleep.

I had detachment issues and I wouldn't let anything go. Babyyy, when I finally did let things go, oh my goodness; it was a whole nother journey. A whole nother level, and a whole nother me. If you're in a space that you're feeling that you cannot accept who you are, or what's happened to you is causing you to feel less than or incomplete, or whatever your case may be, then really sit down and ponder if somebody knew what happened. Then ask, "What they gon' do?" "What they gon' do?" and how is it gon' affect you once you get that kind of attitude about it? You will see a whole nother door open up in your life.

I had to activate an internal thought process to fully accept my truth and know that I can no longer suffer in silence. "What they gon' do? was how I got through so many situations where I would second guess myself. No one else can control me, but me. I had to activate and go deep into who I truly was, and also who I was to become. I always want to become a better version of myself. I enjoy being extra with two scoops of joy; this way I am able to activate the blessings that God has given me to be able to bless others.

It is what it is: Acceptance

- When I worried how my truth would be received by others, it made me feel alone again. I am just as valid as the next person.

- Focusing on everyone's judgment took away a part of the quality of my life. I no longer suffer in silence and live in sovereignty.

FREE resource: go to www.fulfilledandworthy.com select the free resource tab, click Chapter 3.

Cutting ties is not easy, but neither is feeling used. -Angel

Journaling how you successfully overcome emotions and situations will be your blueprint on how to do it again.

-Angel

Chapter 4

"Pressure Release"

S tart the healing process.

How do you handle pressure? When I think of that question, I think of how a pressure cooker sounds when you open it. It takes time for things to cook inside, and when it's done, the sound of the release is refreshing to me. When I reference the infidelity that I experienced in my marriage, the mistreatment as a child, and other unfortunate situations that took place in my life, I think about when I finally released all of that pressure. I recall doing research back then to try and understand how to heal. Some questions that I asked myself were, "Is anyone else going through what I went through? How much time do I need to heal from this? Will I be able to move forward from this happening? What's really causing me to be bothered and feel this

ACTIVATE

way? Can I have a conversation about what happened without blowing up?

Words can also cause quite a bit of pressure. Our words and how we use them can cause pain. I know you've heard the phrase, "sticks and stones may break my bones, but words will never hurt me." LIES! I don't know who came up with that saying, but I don't know who they were trying convence. I'm not sure if they were trying to make a child feel some type of way because somebody has said something bad about them. That saying is a lie all day long. Words may or may not be true, but they do hurt sometimes, they absolutely do.

There was a time when someone's words affected my entire perspective of the person she truly was because the words that she said to me showed me her perspective of me. People will say things such as, "She said that when she was upset, but she didn't mean it." That's not true because when I'm mad, I mean everything I say, I do. Should I have said it the way that I said it? Probably not. However, in my opinion when you're upset, everything that you've thought about a person comes to your remembrance; especially the negative things. There's typically not positive things racing through your mind when you're upset. Like, "oh my gosh, they're so nice. They're so sweet." Absolutely not. It's more like, "that's why your ears are so little and your breath stinks." We instantly go into a negative thought.

It's similar to a protection mechanism.

There is an instance that occurred l when words hurt me more than I realized. I was staying with my maternal grandmother at the time, and I came home from work. I was working at my very first job at KFC. I came home from work and it was around holiday time. I'm not quite sure if it was the holiday itself or that weekend, but there was a gathering at the house where the family gathered to eat, you know, similar to a family cookout.

Well, I came home and my aunt immediately demanded that I go into the kitchen and wash the dishes. I'm looking around a bit confused because I simply wanted to unwind and get in the house. I could've responded to her in so many other ways; however, I decided not to because I am not a disrespectful person. Depending on who you are, that may not always be the case, but I've always tried to respect my elders unless they rubbed me wrong. I was thinking, "I can't even get my shoes off?" Once I looked in the kitchen and I saw the dishes piled up and everywhere, I was infuriated on the inside because I looked around and saw several other candidates who could've washed those dishes. My cousins and other younger family members were there laughing and seemingly having a good time. Besides, I just got off of work and I was exhausted. I refused to wash the dishes at that moment. My auntie said, "Nawl, you gon' wash them now!" I repeated myself as I looked at my auntie, "No, I'm not." Perhaps I would consider washing them later, but I just knew at that moment I wasn't washing them then.

My Auntie then raised her eyebrows, took a breath, and went off on me over the dishes. She literally called me everything, except my name. She even called me a 'drug baby' and more harmful terms. As she was calling me these names, I remember my confusion over why she would react this way over dirty dishes while there were other young people in the house that were capable of washing them. I didn't understand the issue. She then threatened to hit me, and the situation escalated very quickly from there. In hindsight, I don't know what really caused her to be so upset with me. When I think about it more, maybe something happened and she was upset with another family member or boyfriend or whomever, and I just happened to catch the end of it.

Y'all, it got real after she threatened me! It got so real that all I could think of is, "I'm not gonna say too much, and I'm not gonna hit my auntie. But if she hits me, she has to go ahead and put some hammers on me today because I'm going all the way in on her." I was shocked with some of the things that she was saying to me and about me; it was firing me up. Her words were so very hurtful, and everyone heard her. If I didn't already have issues going on, then I definitely would have after what she said. I was closest to my grandma, and I knew she heard her as she was within a few feet of us. She didn't fully intervene, but she may have called her name and asked her to calm down. My Auntie didn't stop. I was hoping that my grandma would step in more aggressively and save me or at least say something else, but that didn't happen either. No one tried to intervene with what was going on. Our argument escalated to the point where I had to leave. As I was walking towards the door, I remember a broom being thrown at me. It didn't hit me, but it was thrown and even more threats were made.

I felt like Cinderella before she knew about the ball. All I could think at that time was that this was over some dishes that several other people could have washed. This was one of my closest aunts at the time. Just to hear the things that she thought of me changed my perception of her. In the end, it changed the whole dynamic of our relationship. I don't think it was ever as great as it was. Don't get me wrong, we are still cool today and we still have good times together, but before that event occurred, you could not see her without seeing me. We were always together. I viewed her as my role model, and I wanted to be just like her at the time.

After that unfortunate event took place, I migrated back to my paternal grandmother, and I would just come and help keep my granddad when needed. When my grandma got home, I would typically go back down to my other grandmother's house.

Reflecting on it now, that was a huge transition of my relationship with my auntie. I also reflected on how my grandma viewed me, or the lack thereof, because she didn't fully intervene. So the saying that 'words don't hurt' is a lie. At times it's also how words are delivered with tone and body language. Let me drop some bars in my own version: Sticks and stones may break my bones, but good delivery and good communication of words will never hurt me. I need to copyright that. Words truly do cause pain, and I had to truly heal from that as I didn't want anything internal to be shown externally.

I recall a time when my mama said to me that I had lost my smile. I asked her, "What do you mean because I smile all of the time." She didn't elaborate on it at that moment, which is shocking because she usually does. However, a couple of years later I know exactly what she meant. In that moment, my healing process and my pressure released. I couldn't hold it anymore. When I finally released everything out, it felt so good. I was relieved from so many things. I had to figure out what was next. In this season I am here to activate the pressure release button to start the healing process. I have laid it out here to let it out while focusing solely on mindset. Thankfully, God brought me through and helped me avoid loads of unwanted stress illnesses. He allowed me to be in a healthy space to have healthy self confidence. Do you have any health related issues that came directly from stress? Do you know how to handle stressful situations?

Focusing solely on activating my mindset, and this helped me avoid a lot of unwanted stress illnesses, as well as allow me to be in a healthy space to have healthy self confidence.

Let it go: Healing

- Do not let the stigma keep you away from healing. I have journeyed through many systems of healing.

- I could not have a conversation without being triggered. I can talk now without re-living pain.

- There are no expectations to overcome internal obstacles. I focused on healing and healing completely. Time has no say.

FREE resource: go to www.fulfilledandworthy.com select the free resource tab, click Chapter 4.

Failure is a part of life, perception is what determines your next move. -Angel

When you're focused on a goal, make sure you have alternate routes to get there.

-Angel

Chapter 5

"Let's Heal" Forgiving it's Healing

Sometimes you gotta just listen. However, at times that's not too easy for someone like me. You know how when your parents tell you not to do something, but you just want to do it so badly because you want to see what would happen? Well, I'll share about a time when my mama clearly told me not to do something, and I did it anyway. Because I did it and she told me not to, I knew she was gonna whoop me. I was gonna get in trouble, trouble, trouble. To avoid getting in trouble, I didn't want to say anything. Here's the story…

I was around 2 or 3 years in age. Back then, we stayed in a trailer and when it was winter time my mom would turn on the stove and open the oven's door to allow heat to warm up the house.

ATTAIN

One night when I was minding my business sitting on the floor, I noticed this bright red light that was so beautiful… y'all know where this is going. I was in a daze just sitting and staring at the glow from that pretty light. Have you ever paid attention to how vibrant the color looks at the bottom of the oven? It was so gorgeous, and it just yelled, "Look at me! Come and touch me!"

While I was looking at the light, the color reminded me of candy, and I wanted to touch it. Obviously my mother clearly told me, "Do not touch this, it's hot. It will hurt you." I don't even know if I responded to her. What I recall is that my mom walked away trusting that I would listen to her direction. As I sat there and I looked at that beaming red glowing light looking back at me, I could hear it summoning me. "How hot can it be?" is what I was thinking. So I inched towards it, looked around to see if mama was around, and then I grabbed it! Yep, sure did! My hand was in a full fist clench around the sizzling device; I grabbed it like it was a popsicle. I burnt my fingers all the way up. My little fingers instantly felt that uncomfortable feeling, and I let it go.

My hand was pounding with pain, and the only thing that I thought that I could do at that moment was to start sweeping my hand on the floor in a back and forth motion as quickly as I could. Almost like you are waving, "Hey girl, hey!" but on the floor. Honey, I was sweeping the floor with that hand as fast as I could trying to sweep the pain away. Now I couldn't cry because Mama's gonna know that I did the one thing that she literally told me not to do. I just had to take that pain. I sat there and that hand was on fire, baby. I know it was. I think about the little iron or curling iron burns that would touch your arm or leg. The oven was hotter.

When my mama came back through the kitchen she said, "Lil' silly girl…what you doin'? Why you sweepin' the flo'?" I just smiled. I didn't say anything, but I couldn't stop sweeping the floor because my hand was hurting so badly. A mother knows her child, so my mother comes over to pick up my hand and she flips it over. "Angel! Oh, my God! What did you do?" She knew in that instant exactly what I had done. I didn't get a whoopin' at that moment, actually I didn't get one at all for what I had done. All I recall is we're off to the emergency room. All was ok. I still have the burn marks to this very day, but the marks are faint. My marks healed, and I acquired wisdom from this unfortunate event.

When I think about this, I ponder that when you're to the point of being so curious that you ignore the facts that someone you trust has told you what will happen, and you just ignore it. Now you have to deal with the consequences. Experience is a good teacher. But honey, let me tell you what I learned. That red means hot, okay, red means stop. Don't go, it's going to burn and your fingers are gonna melt. The bigger thing is that I was so afraid of getting a whoopin' that I wouldn't say anything. If my mother hadn't picked my hand up and looked at it, I don't even know what would have happened. So thank you mama for checking. I love you so much!

When you think about things that people tell you, I recall I used to tell my son 'don't do this', 'don't do that'. When he was younger, he listened, but when he got older I would tell him things, then it was, "Okay Mom, okay Mom" but not really listening. He just wanted me to stop talking to him because we think we know it all at a certain age. We just think we know it all (some of us). Sometimes we gotta go through these experiences to gain wisdom. Well the tables have drastically changed from when I was a little girl till now. My hand healed. I don't want to just gain that wisdom through my own personal experience. Y'all tell me, and I simply want to learn from y'all experiences because I don't want to go through it. It's a 'no' for me. I decided that I can heal through people's experiences.

As I've aged over the years, I've realized that we need to get to the root of any issues in life. Getting to the root will cause healing and will help deal with the issues in your heart. Once your heart is healed, then your identity can change. I remember when I decided to have the conversation with my parents about my feelings, and why I felt the way I felt to just seek for some understanding. I was curious to see if they could shed some light on it for me.

I remember it so vividly when I told my mama that I wanted to have a talk with her about the past and my childhood. My mama is the no nonsense mama. She has a limited filter and typically is not worried about your feelings. She will tell you how it is 100%. It is what it is. She's the type of mama that will 'cut you down'. I love this about her. She doesn't have bad intentions, but she's coming from a place of reacting with what her life has given her. So the closer and closer it came to the moment for me to talk to her, the faster my heart started beating and the more nervous I became. I was a grown woman over 40 years old and felt like the 8 year old abused little girl at that moment. It was like the space was getting smaller and smaller as I walked to her to start the conversation.

My heart was literally racing.

So the time has now approached, and I need to start the conversation with my mama. We've had a lot of uncomfortable conversations before, however, this one by far was the hardest one for me. I realized at that moment that I did not want to hurt her feelings or make her feel bad for any of the decisions or choices that she was forced to make back then. So I tried to approach it in the manner of 'I've been dealing with some things and I was wondering if you could help me out'.

As we had the conversation, I explained to her how I was struggling with not being loved and feeling abandoned as a child and wanting to know why things happened the way they did back then. At that moment, I stared into my mama's eyes and I felt like crying. I could see how the memories and reality were hurting her. I knew that it was never her intention to make me feel that way. She likely never thought about how it would affect me later in life, younger years or older.

As always, she told me her truth and as uncomfortable as it was to see my mother in that space, I needed to see that. She shared that she was simply not in a mental or emotional place to be the fit mother that her kids deserved. She had some addictions that she couldn't release, but she absolutely loved us and wanted what was best for us.

I needed to hear those words. I needed to know that she cared and that how I felt mattered to her. I wanted to feel validated by her, and I did. I respect my mama so much. She did the best she could with the cards she was dealt. This conversation was a really big turning point in my relationship with my mama. I am a mama, and as a mama, you never leave your own mama. This is the person who you've always been able to rely on regardless of what ups and downs you may have had in the past. That moment was probably one of the best moments of my life with my mama.

I then approached my father to have the same conversation. My daddy and I didn't talk much and when we did, it was almost as if I was a disciplinarian because that was just my demeanor. This was how we communicated, however, with this particular topic I felt like the air was disappearing around me again as I approached him. My hands were sweating. As I tried to calm down and relax and tried to control my breathing, that didn't help. I was so nervous and so afraid of what his response was going to be. But again, I needed to know for myself. My father was a man of few words at times. I knew it was not a conversation that he would be comfortable having, but if I caught him at the right time, at the right moment, then I felt that he would share with me or at least be okay with having the conversation.

So as I looked at my dad in his eyes with a cracking voice, I mustered up the nerve to ask him why? The response I received was not the one that I expected to have, however, I knew it was his truth. "When you know better, you do better." As the tears filled my daddy's eyes, the biggest tears began to run down his face, and in that moment I forgot all about me and my issues. I could see all of the issues that he was carrying just as much. I could feel the regret, but also the love that he has for his children. The conversation didn't last long.

We ended the emotional conversation with a hug and 'I love you's'. As I was driving home that evening, all I could do was think about what he could have felt. The entire experience encouraged me to talk to other people. I know that these types of conversations will yield to even more questions. I had to think about how much weight does this carry in my life? When situations occur, we usually want to know their 'Why'? Why did you do it? Why did this happen? Why did you allow this? My response was a question that came back, and it was, "Does their why really matter?" Then I wanted to know is this affecting them at all? Or is it just me? That led to thoughts of why am I allowing it to affect me this way? Do I even have any control over it?

I realized a few things, such as holding on is only hurting and holding me back from my next levels of happiness. More questions came up, you know, and I think these were probably some of the biggest questions that anyone going through a healing process can ask themselves. Have I forgiven myself? What am I holding over my own head? What do I do about it?

What I learned through this is that not addressing things earlier allows issues to build up. Holding on allows you to create your own truth. Holding on only allows you to be stuck in that moment. Now as time went on, I reflected on the conversations that I had with my parents, and sometimes I think about what understanding came from it. I think about their lives at that moment. What was the best choice for them and if it hadn't been different, would it really matter? I think about all the other situations they were dealing with at work, with other family members judging them, and also self blame.

These are things that I'll never really know. But it doesn't really matter because this is where I'm at now. I am in a good space, thankfully. I had to address things for myself because doing the things that I needed to do for myself helped me truly be able to forgive some situations that I never thought I could forgive. Some things I never thought that I could release, but I was able to. I had to hit a reset and change my perspective. I had to stop feeling sorry for myself. The past is the past and I cannot change that, but I can control my future and my decisions. I had to acquire the courage to move forward.

Nothing else in the past has mattered. My parents did what they did, whether it was with good intentions or not, it happened. Here we are now, how do we move forward? My communication changed with them. I became more trusting of the things that I wanted to say to them. It's okay to say what you need to say. Just say it in the correct manner. You don't have to be disrespectful about it. That was one thing that I did. Sometimes if I thought that it was going to be really or borderline disrespectful, I may write it down. Beforehand, read it a couple of times, maybe reword it to see which way is gonna work best. I chose to reflect on things more. I knew that if I didn't let things go, then I would never be able to move forward.

In this season, we are here to attain emotional trust or self trust. I had to forgive myself for all the things that I blamed myself for, and I had to attain forgiveness to all the people through first acknowledging that the things happened out loud or through journaling. I also had to accept what happened to me. Again, that acceptance came through talking to trusted family/friends and counselors. But by doing this allowed me to start the process of trusting myself more.

Increasing my quality of life: Foregiving

- During the majority of my life I would suffer from migraines. When I started forgiving and letting go of my anger, the migraines stopped.

- I just hold tight to hurt and pain. It just held me back from my happiness and future.

- I was so angry about my pain, because I would not accept it. I embrace the experience and process of emotional pain healing.

FREE resource: go to www.fulfilledandworthy.com select the free resource tab, click Chapter 5.

CHAPTER 6

"GOTTA LOVE ME" SELF LOVE JOURNEY

Have you ever heard the saying that you can catch more flies with honey than you can vinegar? That phrase has never meant more to me until I really understood what they were saying. You attract what you put out, and flies like the sweet stuff. If you want the flies, then you have to put the sweet stuff out there. However, if you had your vinegar out there, then you wouldn't attract the flies because flies don't like vinegar. Learning, walking in, and understanding that you really attract what you put out, which is also known as the law of attraction, is the same thing, but it's apparent that it works. If you don't know any better, then you can't do any better.

ATTAIN

When you truly have the people that care about you, they'll tell you what's going on the entire time. They'll give you little tidbits and cues here and there. You just got to pick up on context clues. I haven't always been so good at picking up on context clues because I haven't always paid much attention. My entire life was about everyone else, and I felt that I had to put everyone else before me. I'm not complaining about it, but it was my reality. It was positioned that my siblings were my responsibility, and I was to take care of them. Therefore, I did through adulthood.

I also was responsible for watching over my granddaddy when I was in high school. He was ill and bedridden. After school I would feed him, clean him up, give him fluids to stay hydrated, help him move from the chair to the bed, as well as anything else that he needed. Since this was my daily routine after school, I would miss out on some of the celebratory engagements. Okay, let me just call them for what they are– parties or games. I missed out on so many events. I truly became a servant. It was about making sure everybody else had what they needed, and not ever really knowing what I needed or what I wanted. I didn't even realize that I was supposed to desire a need for myself.

My childhood best friend would always say, "You gotta do it for you. You've got to learn to love yourself. You've got to take care of yourself." But in my mind taking care of me was taking care of everyone else because it was my job. After hearing it for a while I wanted to love myself so I started trying to do things that I thought would work. I thought it was things like going to get your nails done, or going get your hair done, buying a new outfit because those things make you feel good.

When you look good, you feel good. That was the type of mindset that I had because that's what I heard people say. Everyone of my best friends would continue to encourage me to do something for myself, but I didn't know what that was. I would convince them that I did because I had gotten my nails done. It didn't make me feel differently. I mean, yeah, it was cute. My nails were poppin'. When I got my hair done, my hair was slayed. I could go put on one of those outfits, but nothing was enough. There was still a void. On the inside I still felt empty. How did you learn to do something that you've never been taught to do? How do you learn to do something when you don't even feel like you're worthy of that?

Throughout life I would see that if you're not important to yourself, then no one else is going to make you a priority or they're not gonna care either. I got to a point where I felt like I had this love thing down, I felt like I had a lot. When I realized that it wasn't that I didn't love myself, it was just that I was taught to love others more or I held them in a higher regard than I held myself. I was so used to being put on the back burner.

When you're used to something being your norm and you've done it for years, then that's hard to come out of it.

I remember the first time I felt self love, and what it really felt like. This occurred when I put myself out there for love and I moved in with the guy I was dating, the new Boo. We had all of these plans on being together. I ignored all of the red flags that I saw and felt prior to moving in with him. He had just purchased a home and I assisted him with furniture and decorations. We were quickly building a life together.

About a month later, one of my best friends invited me to a weekend seminar. Our birthday is around the same time, so you know we are Virgos, and we are great and wanted to celebrate together. I was telling the boyfriend at the time that I wanted to go to the event and informed him that I had been invited. I explained to him that our birth birthdays were in the same month and we try to do something together around that time frame. Sometimes it's a little earlier, sometimes it's later when we are able to celebrate. That part can vary, but we always celebrate our birthdays together in some way. We've been doing it for a few years now.

He didn't want me to go. I contemplated not going based on his initial response. I hesitated, but told my best friend that I wasn't sure if I would go, and I would let her know. As the days passed, something kept pushing me to go to this event. I needed to attend this event. I felt it internally that I really needed to go. Then, I finally told him that I'd decided that I wanted to attend the event. His response was so out of left field. He said that he didn't want me to go, and he had his reasons. His reasons were not valid at all, nor were they true. I told him I understood and heard what he said, however, I still wanted to attend the event. After I said that to him, I can literally remember his exact words, and it was as if it was in slow play.

He said, "If you go, we are done."

I was so shocked at what he said. I needed to make sure that I heard him correctly. "Wait, what?" I asked for clarity. He repeated himself. I took a pause and tried to process what I just heard. He was serious. I knew that I was going to the event, and I shared that my mind was made up about it. He then said, "Well, if you're going, then we can end it now. You can get out." I was very hurt and in disbelief, like are you serious right now? I live here, what do you mean get out? He repeated himself again calmly, "You can get out." I shared with him that his words were very hurtful and to please be mindful and understand what you're requesting of me. You can't take back things that you say. Well, by the third time he said it was really more forceful. "You can get out!"

I simply got up in my gown, slipped my slides on, grabbed a set of my car keys and told him I'll be back to get my stuff tomorrow. As I pulled away, I realized I was homeless. I had sold everything and relocated with him. That was the first time that I ever did anything like that. I am also pretty sure it'll be the last time too. The only way that this type of occurrence will happen is if the good Lord puts in on my spirit, and that will be a real hard prayer.

So, I went home, which was about an eight and a half hour drive away. My best friend was out of town at the time. I asked her if I could stay with her for a few days? I didn't really want to tell her what was going on; I wanted her to enjoy her moment.

The weekend event changed my life forever. All I had were the clothes on my back. The now ex boyfriend wouldn't allow me to get my items without practically begging him; so I was forced to leave everything behind. I mean everything. I tried to get my items with the police and a facilitator; however, that failed. I left everything behind.

While I was at the event, I felt the presence of the Lord move boldly. I was receiving so much. I realized that for the first time in my life, I chose me. I chose me. I chose me, and that was the best feeling in the world. I had to process how I felt about the decision that I made. The decision that I made yielded immediate actions. Regardless of what it was, I had to put myself first and it's not an easy thing to do if you're not used to doing it. Heck, I still struggle with it sometimes. I don't always get it right, but when I realize that I'm not making myself a priority, the whole energy will change. As I started to make myself a priority, so did others.

When you realize that you are the priority, then never do anything that makes you feel less than. This is a different level of self love. Loving yourself is a different kind of self power because it takes discipline. It wasn't always easy. It's hard to say no. It's hard to not do something that you know that you can do. However, it's also good to not feel used and not feel like you're being taken advantage of. I chose to be the 'uncomfortable no' versus the 'miserable yes'. What's your choice?

There are certain change agents or steps to change. The first thing is being aware of it. You have to own it. You have to admit it. How many people do you know that they need to (or say they want to) lose weight or know that they may not be in their normal space or know that they need to stop smoking and drinking. A factor to why they don't is because they hadn't really accepted or acknowledged that there is a real problem. Another factor could be the reasoning behind why they need to accomplish the chosen goal, and the "why" is not important enough for them to make a change.

My next step would be analyzing how you can incorporate small changes that you can stick to. I started on so many projects so many times, and stopped and started over, and stopped and started over, and stopped and started over. You get the picture. Heck, I even did it with this book if I'm being transparent. There are times when I just jumped into something (can we say impulsive), I didn't really stop or take the time to see what I could really handle that would allow me to be successful at whatever that venture was. Almost like taking baby steps; just one step, then another step, or the third step is to just see movement. Procrastination is real. Procrastination will sneak in on you quicker than you think while you're saying I could be doing this, this, this, this or this. I know it doesn't just happen to me. You must move on it and strike when the iron is hot as the saying goes. Are you a procrastinator?

There were many times I knew what to try, or what I thought I should try or maybe even what I thought I should do. However, I never put forth the effort to do it. Procrastination! I never jumped on it and was like do it, do it, go, go. No, no, no. I just procrastinate. So avoid procrastination and move instantly. When you think about it, act. When you say it, do it. When you talk about it, respond to it. Still be mindful of how you're able to incorporate these new changes in your life and how you're going to work around them, if you find a hiccup.

The next step is knowledge. Equip yourself with the knowledge that you need to know to be successful. Don't worry about it. I got you. I've been living this for years and I've completed tons of research on it. Experience is a good teacher, now I've lived through it. I went through the steps, and I know that they work. After I wrote this book, I relived all of the things that I talked about. I felt that was God's way of confirming some things for me and making sure that what I speak works. Also, I needed confirmation that I had healed from it. Your step by step plan (knowledge) is critical because that is going to set you up whether you're going to be successful, or whether you're going to fail.

Let me give you an example. There was one thing that I read at one point that said, "Every morning you need to get up and you need to exercise 30 minutes in the morning." In my mind, I thought that I could do it. Well, guess what? The first three or four days, I was on it. However, on day five something came up, and I couldn't get to it. Then on day six, something else came up. Well, guess what? By day seven, I had probably given up on it. When I took on that initiative, I truly knew I wasn't a morning person. I didn't take the time to research enough to look at other options that may have been better for me. I just thought that I could do it. I cheered myself on internally with, "Girl you got this, you can do it!" But deep down I knew that I was not a morning person. I knew how long it took me to get ready for work in the mornings. Then came the excuses, I have to do this or I gotta do that. The reality was evenings and nights were better for me. I wanted to believe that I could do it, but I was not realistic with myself. Now I'm sure I could have done it, my why was just not strong enough at that time. That wasn't what I desired to do at the time.

Also I had somewhat of a pride issue, and I didn't ask for guidance. I didn't ask for help. I wanted to do it on my own. I even went back and forth on the fact that I didn't want to be prideful, but I couldn't say I was embarrassed because I don't get easily embarrassed about things. But sometimes I'm too proud to ask for help or I've asked for help before and didn't get it, so I just figured I'll do it alone. Now let me be clear and transparent. There's nothing wrong with doing it alone. As long as you're disciplined, get guidance and you know what steps to take. Be okay with starting over. If the first route that you take doesn't work, be okay with that.

The approach that I take in this life now is to deep dive into learning a little bit more about what your lifestyle is as well as what your likes and what your dislikes are. We can then come up with something that's realistic for you to start. We may have to make adjustments along the way, and that's okay. As long as we continue to see progress, then we will get to the finish line.

Now that you have the knowledge, it's time for us to take action. We can't just talk about it, we have to get on it. Action! At times, there was no accountability partner for a lot of things that I've done. If I'm being honest, when I did get an accountability partner, so much stuff hit my plate so many excuses or reasons were falling in my lap. I had so much doubt. Let's call it for what it is. Even though I felt that I could push through the doubt, during this particular time I was struggling, remember the point when I mentioned that I struggle to ask for help? I did get the courage one day to ask for help, and the help I received didn't actually help me. So they pushed me back and I sat in and I just kept coming up with different excuses. But I didn't give up, I just needed a work around because I'm gonna get it.

I've learned through this journey if it's for you, baby nobody else can have it. That's what I had to keep telling myself. I know what God has told me. It's for me. It's up to me to work to go get it, and he's gonna make the way. I wasn't working, let me clarify that I wasn't doing enough work. I was going through some motions, but that was just to be able to say that I tried or completed a little bit. One good thing about taking action is that you can look at it as if it's an experiment. If course A doesn't work, we'll just try course B and we'll keep trying different courses until we find the one that works. Sometimes people forget that a lot of things are trial and error. Sometimes we get it right the first time, and sometimes we don't. Sometimes what happens, which is what happened to me with this book, is when you take action you go back to contemplation or you end up back in step one. Then we need to focus on step two, step three, and now we have some action. Now we are in the cycle that just repeats itself, and sometimes it happens that way before you complete it. That was my story. I don't want it to be yours. You must acquire what you need.

What I did discover as I kept going back to step one of acknowledging was that when I hit my knowledge stage, I missed something. I missed something that I needed to completely push me from the action step to the completion step. Therefore, I needed to do more research, and I did it along with prayer. When you have to go back to step one, many people look at that as failure and they give up as opposed to understanding that there was just a piece of the knowledge puzzle that was missed.

One of my biggest components that I knew was that I wasn't being fully honest with myself. There was a component in my lifestyle that I hadn't worked out yet. I did in certain areas, but not in totality. What I was doing was still putting some of the people that I loved needs before mine.

Their fires became my fires, and through prayer and meditation, and many instances of hurt feelings, I had to come to realize that I have to make my fires my own. No one cared about my fires as much as I did. No one cared about my fires like I cared about their fires. Then the even harsher reality of it was that I had to stop expecting them. These were the relationship expectations that I had allowed to be created. Accepting this was a real struggle for me. Treat others how you want to be treated, and I do. But the part that I didn't get was don't expect others to treat you as you treat them. Once I fully understood that, I got back into step one, and I started moving.

One of the last stages, to me, is self accountability. When you can get to the point of self accountability is when you've mastered that stage. If you can hold yourself accountable, then you can do what you desire to do. The self accountability aspect will have you working out when you are on vacation. It will have you praying in front of your friends or moving to a private place to pray. Accountability will have you excusing yourself because it matters to you by the time you reach this stage. Then, whatever habits or whatever goals you are working on has become part of you. It has become what you desire to do, which is different when you do something because you want to and not because you have to. Therefore, you enjoy it more. It matters more to you. You do it with no regrets.

I don't know about y'all, but when I need to go work out, I go just because I need to. I mean, I'm gonna be cute or whatever, but I'm probably not gonna give it my all, let's just be real. I'm not. I'm still waiting for somebody to create something (outside of surgery) that I believe in, so I don't have to. Okay, okay, I know that sounds bad, but it's true. I know that I've got to work out. I get it, I get it. I'm gonna do it. But I'm gonna do it on my terms the way that I want to because I'll do it more. If I had to put it into another perspective, think about things that you want to do. Nobody has to ask you to do it. Nobody has to tell you to do it, it's done because you want to. No one has to beg you. When you want to do something, it is done, when you have to do something, it's a different feeling. You take your time, you lollygag and it's just most of the time you half do it. Let's call it for what it really is. Now, when it's something that you want, you are going to do it right.

I'll give you a better example. I'm an organizer. I love everything to have a visual essence and a visual presentation. It's gotta look good. At the time that I a, writing this book, I'm organizing a pantry. Nobody has to tell me to get up to go and organize the pantry because I want to. On the other hand, when I'm trying to get my kids to help me, for example, lining the cabinets in the kitchen, oh my gosh, let me tell you those liners are short and some are too long. The liners are crooked just tossed in there any kind of way. Now, not all my kids, just the ones that don't want to do it. Now I have one who enjoys the kind of organization I like to do. Just call her my mini me. But the rest of them, nope. I know that if I asked them to do it and they're doing it because they have and I'm going to end up redoing it, then I don't even ask them. What are some things that you do but you don't enjoy? What is something if you could change it, that would make you enjoy it.

One of the biggest challenges that I had in this self love journey was learning how to establish healthy boundaries.

This is similar to showing people how to treat you because if you allow it, they will do it. What I learned through creating healthy boundaries is simply saying something along the lines of, "Hey, I don't like it when you talk to me like that. If you continue to talk in this manner, then we are not going to be able to continue to have conversations." At first, I thought that was really hard to do. I thought that it sounded bad. However, it actually works if they respect you enough and they want to be a part of your life and have a healthy relationship with you. They'll respect what you're saying. Respect yourself more and create healthy boundaries.

In this season I had to attain tools to ensure that I was loving myself, and it's a journey. This was attained by talking through the issues and speaking life (affirmations) over the things that I needed release from. I even wrote letters about some things and claimed release over them. It's still a journey day by day. This journey is something I must be intentional about. I now desire to put myself and my feelings first; this has been beneficial and a healthy practice.

If I do not value me, how can I expect others to: Self Trust

- When I did not set boundaries, I felt invisible. When I became aware of how my actions would ignite my triggers, I now prioritize my self worth first.

- You attract what you put out. I protect my mental space and mind by being intentional on the type of people I am surrounding myself with even to what I watch and see.

- I used to think something is better than nothing. I confidently value all parts of me physically, mentally, emotionally, and most importantly giving myself grace.

FREE resource: go to www.fulfilledandworthy.com select the free resource tab, click Chapter 6.

Learn to be okay in the silence in between. -Angel

Chapter 7

"Happily Moving Forward" How to maintain in this space

This chapter could be a whole book by itself, but there were things that were taught during our adolescence, such as our childhood beliefs or ways of living that you simply adapted to. It's natural because that's what you were taught. That's what you grew up believing to be true, and that was it without question. Now, some of those beliefs are somewhat null and void and no longer apply. However, you're so committed to it that you can't move. Let's just talk about it. I've already mentioned that I was taught that crying is a sign of weakness. You don't cry. You don't let anyone see you cry. I also mentioned that I was taught that you don't get a divorce; you stick it out regardless. I was also taught and told to not separate children. You don't separate your family no matter what. I was taught that what goes on in this house stays in this house. Another childhood lesson was to not bother anybody with your problems. Those are just to name a few.

I previously mentioned that I am a very literal person. I am very black and white. For example, if you give me directions, then I'm going to follow those directions step by step.For this reason, I am good at putting furniture together that comes with directions. I'm not going to take directions away, but I may add to it (extra, you know that's me). I'm going to put my own splash of flavor on it. However, it was always to help increase versus decrease.

Many of the beliefs I was taught as a kid led me to make terrible decisions in adulthood. When you know better, you do better just like my daddy taught me. I am very guilty of not making my problem somebody else's problem; very guilty of it. I have improved upon it, but I still have a little bit more of that to work out. Now I'm intentional with it.

That phrase, "What goes on in his house stays in his house" still rings in households now. At one point I didn't think that it affected my life so much as not separating the kids and not having a lot of baby fathers. I still abided by that one the most. But the one that caused the most elapsed time in my life was the notion that you don't get a divorce. I can remember my grandmother saying to us, "The way he is now is who he is. He's not going to change. So if you say yes to the now, then you have to stick to it later." That belief caused me to stay in my marriage way longer than I should have. But what really triggered me to be open to unlearn those beliefs is how it was presented to me. It took one of my best friends putting it in a different perspective for me. So I will say it again, it's good to have somebody to talk to. That was then, but this is now. It was basically like this, "You were raised by your grandparents, therefore, the things that they grew up in and the things that were happening in that day and age, which was well over 90 plus years ago now, doesn't apply to how life evolved and how things are in today's current age" she shared. That resonated with me and that made sense.

I could think about how back then when I was singing all those songs, that nobody loved me. My silent cry for somebody to help me, no one would have thought to say, "hey, you know, let's go get her mental health checked out." Mental health wasn't a thing back then. "Be quiet! Adults are talking now, go in the room, sit down, and shut up." That's what I grew up hearing repeatedly; therefore, that was my reality. "When adults are talking you don't talk, and when I tell you something you don't question me" are more phrases I remember from childhood.

Nothing back then in my world was like today's society. That made sense to me. Again, until it was presented to me in a way that I related to, I was not able to see why that system was expired and faulty. So having to unlearn the things that you may have been raised on even though it came from a family member that you trust and would give everything for, that's just not it.

It's all about personal growth, personal development, self awareness, self accountability, self love, getting a counselor, and over everything and putting yourself first. So unlearning those things helped me move into a new space. You may have heard the saying, "you gotta make it make sense." Once it makes sense and you agree with it, it's a lot easier to understand.

I am happily moving forward now. I am finally at the point of space of loving myself and owning my voice. You can too. So now you may ask yourself these questions: What do you do? What do you do with this voice?

As the days go by, I'm trying to process these new sets of emotions and feelings that I have. I do not want to lose these feelings nor ever go back to the uncomfortable space that I experienced before when I constantly second guessed myself. I would ask myself, "What did I actually do to get here?" At that point, I knew that I needed to write everything down. My thoughts, emotions, feelings, and everything simply needed to be written down. As I started writing about how I can stay in this space, I was realizing and writing down the things that make me happy and bring me joy. It felt so good to write them down too. I realized that when I do things of self expression, such as writing, painting, singing, dancing, and things of that nature, it keeps my mind in a good space and keeps me better for everything else. This space I am in also keeps me in control. Anything that feels good to my soul I can do, but not at the point of me feeling less than.

I remember the first time I had to tell someone "No." I could barely muster the words out of my mouth. I knew I had to and my new practice was actually to say no to everything. It doesn't matter how it makes you feel, it doesn't matter what it is. Just say no. Get used to saying no. It was almost as if 'no' wasn't even in my vocabulary. My thought process was that you can't just do it one time and stop because old habits won't die. They go into hibernation and wait for the opportunity to pop out when triggered or allowed.

I knew that I had to go to a season of isolation. At one point, my family really meant so much to me that I didn't take job offers and I didn't want to move. I didn't want to do anything because they were my first priority, even if I wasn't theirs. They were my everything, they were all that I knew and were my comfort. I couldn't imagine life without being in close proximity to them 'just in case'.

But man, if you don't know that God has a sense of humor, he does! What he did for me was he put it to where somebody just as important to me as my family was, needed me just as much, and I couldn't say no to her either. So what do you do when you can't say no to two people? The things you can't say no to are tearing you apart. He made me an offer that I couldn't resist. I said, "Lord if this happens smoothly, then I'll leave. I'll go and I'll do this." Well, he made me an offer that I couldn't turn down. You know they say God will put you in places that you can't imagine. Well, He will and He did. I'm a testimony to that, but we will save that for another book and another day.

What happened was I had to relocate out of town. I had to move to a city with no friends, and I had to go through a season of isolation. When I was in this season of isolation I started to see things a lot clearer. It was very uncomfortable for me. There were a lot of tears to the point where I was told to stop initiating everything to everybody and see what happens. I was like, "but you know I talk to my mom, my sister, my son, and my best friends everyday! What do you mean? But in this season, I knew some things were being cut away and doors were being opened. Therefore, I had to be obedient and walk through those doors. I said to myself, "Okay, here goes nothing!"

Crickets.

I barely got any calls or any texts. Then I realized that I was putting in all the work to make my desired relationships work. If I didn't initiate it, then it barely happened. In that moment, I was able to see how I truly felt undervalued by anybody, but myself. I can't fully say undervalued by anybody because I had a couple of people that were in touch, but overall it was crickets. I then had to realize and ask myself if I really want the relationship that bad to where I'm willing to initiate our communication efforts. I think my initiations were happening so much that it was what was expected from everyone. That's what it became; which was a very hurtful season.

Can you imagine realizing that if you don't reach out to people that you feel like you're the closest to and love the most don't think about you as much as you think about them? I had to start self reflecting and create your daily routine. In this daily routine, I would celebrate myself. Whatever that looked like, I would celebrate myself and think about how I could speak life into me. That became part of my daily routine. Doing something that makes me happy became part of my routine.

You have to find out what works for you. Make the time for you each day where you can focus on yourself for 30 minutes to two hours at least five days a week. You can control more than you know, and one of the biggest hurdles that I had to overcome was being comfortable with being okay to celebrate myself. It's okay! Protect your energy. You know they say you attract what you put out, but if they aren't putting out what you want, then give them what they give you. There's a saying that states, "don't be mad when I give you the same energy that you're giving me?"

Protect your space. Celebrate yourself and watch what happens. I had to learn how to set healthy boundaries, which includes saying no and sticking to it. Lastly, be open to healthy relationships and expect good things in spite of the past.

Throughout the seven seasons and chapters in this book, I had to remain in the maintenance phase of happily moving forward. This allowed me to accomplish healthier relationships because I was no longer bitter and I was no longer suffering in silence. I acknowledged the situations that happened, and was able to talk about them more. I reached the point where I could accept my truth and walk in it. I hit my rock bottom, and that led to my pressure release. I then came to a point where I had to understand that forgiving is not for the other person. Forgiveness is for me. Therefore, I was able to forgive freely and let go of unfortunate occurrences from the past. I began the self love journey which birthed my ability to trust the decisions that I made. As it pertains to attaining healthy relationships, I felt abandoned as a child. I felt unwanted, unloved, and helpless at times, which carried over into my adulthood. I experienced seven seasons throughout the seven chapters of this book, and what I was able to accomplish has been maintained. The formula is assisting, activating, acquiring and attaining. This practice has led me to feel fulfilled and worthy. You can feel the same way.

Moving on and no looking back: Owning and Maintaining

- I am adopting in this new space. I am doing whatever keeps me feeling good to my soul, but not at the point that I feel less than.

- Structuring my environment is critical. I ensure that I have affirmations, accountability and support through each and every day. I accept that this is what I need and I am ok with having it.

FREE resource: go to www.fulfilledandworthy.com select the free resource tab, click Chapter 7.

It's okay to be proud of things that you're good at. - Angel

Taking care of everyone else while personally settling for less will only cause regret.

-Angel

Closing/Epilogue:

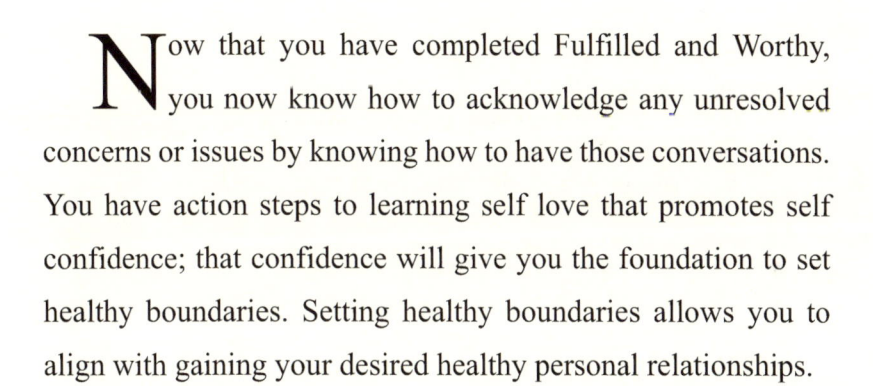

—•◦•—

Now that you have completed Fulfilled and Worthy, you now know how to acknowledge any unresolved concerns or issues by knowing how to have those conversations. You have action steps to learning self love that promotes self confidence; that confidence will give you the foundation to set healthy boundaries. Setting healthy boundaries allows you to align with gaining your desired healthy personal relationships.

Now that you know which actions to take, it's time to get started. If you did not work through action steps as you were reading the chapters, I want to go back to each chapter starting with chapter one and complete each step so you can get your journey started. This journey will change your mindset. You will see a shift in your personal perception of yourself and your personal views. You will see a difference in how others interact with you, treat you and you will feel better about the relationships you have. You may be uncomfortable in the beginning, but there will be situations that you have to recall, and emotions that will need to be processed. You will have to do some self reflection, apply self-discipline practices, and trust yourself. Along the journey, you will become your priority, feel confident in your decisions, learn to stick to your 'No's, and accept what makes you happy. Your journey starts today.

In this book, you learned strategies to help you Acknowledge, Activate, Attain & Align to become Fulfilled & Worthy.

Here's a brief breakdown:

- Chapter one "No One Can Know" you learned that you're not alone and how to internal acknowledge your story, owning your voice.

- Chapter two "Okay, It Happened" you've learned to externally acknowledge that it happened and now it is time to talk about how to allow yourself to start the self love journey.

- Chapter three "What They Gon' Do?" you learned how to accept your truth and own what happened, which activates the healing process.

- Chapter four "Pressure Release" provided how to let go of built up or past emotions that activates your self confidence.

- Chapter five "Let's Heal" you learned how to attain emotional (self) trust through forgiveness.

- Chapter six "Gotta Love Me" you learned how to embrace your self love journey and understand how to attain healthy boundaries.

- Chapter seven "Happily Moving Forward" you learn once you've aligned with your desired space how to maintain this new space.

I want you to move forward and use these strategies so you, too, can align to becoming Fulfilled and Worthy, and gain the healthy personal relationships that you desire. Don't let this book be another unused book on a shelf. I learned self love, acknowledged a boost of confidence, activated and attained self trust, and was able to align with my desired relationships by using the 4 A's. These actions can help you as well. Walk on the self love journey with me if I can do it, so can you! If you find yourself struggling to take the first step, let me show you how through guided support. If nothing changes, then nothing will change. You are stronger than you know. ~Angel Tennelle

- » If you would like me to speak at any event please contact me via email: worthy@angeltennelle.com

- » If you would like to join the email/text list to receive free resources and any upcoming events go to www.fulfilledandworthy.com and click the "stay in the know" tab.

- » If you want to join the fulfilled and worthy Facebook family, then go to Facebook and request to join there.

- » If you still have something missing, want more, lack self love, or desire healthy personal relationships and want details becoming fulfilled and worthy, go to <u>www.fulfilledandworthy.com</u> and click request info tab

I've learned to love who loves me. -Angel

Acknowledge, Activate, Attain & Align. Becoming Fulfilled & Worthy!

Most of my life, I was not being true to myself, not truly understanding who I was, struggling to find my voice, my place in life, and I had little to no self value and existed in unhealthy relationships. However, with my success at work on a continuous upward trajectory, my well maintained lifestyle, and my happy image of family life made me appear fulfilled. My smile hid it all! The harsh truth is, I felt stuck. I was lonely, unhappy, angry, ashamed, becoming emotionally detached, still traumatized from childhood abandonment, but I desired more out of life. Which of these feelings can you relate to? Are you feeling stuck? Do you desire more in life?

Once I hit a breaking point, it forced me to face my fears and make some changes. Fulfilled and Worthy provides simple strategies that will help you acknowledge and learn self love, activate or reactivate self confidence, activate and attain self trust while setting guilt free boundaries, and align with the healthy personal relationships that you desire.

- Work out unresolved emotions
- Own your voice
- Accept and love the skin you're in
- Learn to set healthy boundaries
- Become open to receive the relationships you desire
- Maintain this new mental space
- Choose yourself

You will increase self love, improve self worth, welcome your truth, develop healthy relationships, appreciate boundaries, and gain what makes you feel fulfilled.

Angel Tennelle is a native of Bolivar, TN. She has lived outside of Nashville in a city called Murfreesboro for the last 20 years. She has been training and coaching on a professional level for over 22 years. Her passion to help others learn and grow has allowed her to develop students, employees and leaders through various teaching methods to reach the desired goals. Angel is full of joy and always says "When God was giving out joy, he gave her 2 scoops!" To get more guided resources or additional assistance, visit www.angeltennelle.com.